THE CARELESS SEAMSTRESS

African
POETRY
BOOK SERIES

Series editor: Kwame Dawes

THE CARELESS SEAMSTRESS

Tjawangwa Dema

Foreword by Kwame Dawes

University of Nebraska Press / Lincoln and London

Acknowledgments for the use of copyrighted
material appear on page xvii, which constitutes
an extension of the copyright page.

The African Poetry Book Series has been made
possible through the generosity of philanthropists
Laura and Robert F. X. Sillerman, whose
contributions have facilitated the establishment
and operation of the African Poetry Book Fund.

Library of Congress Cataloging-in-Publication Data
Names: Dema, Tjawangwa, author.
Title: The careless seamstress / Tjawangwa
Dema; foreword by Kwame Dawes.
Description: Lincoln: University of Nebraska
Press, [2019] | Series: African poetry book
series | Includes bibliographical references.
Identifiers: LCCN 2018043032
ISBN 9781496214126 (pbk.: alk. paper)
ISBN 9781496215307 (epub)
ISBN 9781496215314 (mobi)
ISBN 9781496215321 (pdf)
Classification: LCC PR9408.B683 D46 2019
| DDC 821/.92—dc23 LC record available
at https://lccn.loc.gov/2018043032.

Set in Garamond Premier by E. Cuddy.

For mama and papa

CONTENTS

FOREWORD

Kwame Dawes

Many of us have been looking forward to this debut collection from Tjawangwa Dema. I certainly have since I met her several years ago and since I toured with her and a most brilliant cluster of African poets through southern Africa. Dema's command of the stage, her clarity of ideas, and her quick and learned wit in conversation and in her poems begged the question of why she was not published. She was generous enough to allow the African Poetry Book Fund to publish her first chapbook, *Mandible*, as part of the inaugural series of chapbook box sets, *Seven New Generation African Poets: A Chapbook Box Set*, which included an impressive group of poets who are effectively charting a new path for African poetry—Ladan Osman, Tsitsi Jaji, Len Verwey, Clifton Gachagua, Nick Makoha, and Warsan Shire. After several years of intense writing, touring, and completing a graduate degree in creative writing, TJ Dema's first full-length collection, *The Careless Seamstress*, is in your hands. The wait has been worth it.

Anchoring this remarkable debut of poems is the elegy "In the House of Mourning," in which Dema brilliantly and insightfully observes, "Everyone rehearses death, / at nightfall." One has the sense that she has offered us an aphorism of deep wisdom that is immensely quotable for its structure, its clarity, and its complexity. Indeed, her collection enacts this rehearsal of death—not because the poems are morbid and heavy with death (they are not), but because the poems are not fearful of considering the stark truth of our existence, which is framed by birth and death. This awareness is the beginning of wisdom, and, as it happens, the beginning of beauty. Like many of the poems in the collection, all conversations seem to return to the mother, and one imagines that mother to be Dema's mother. In some poems, her mother is identified clearly as such, and in other poems, she seems to be an addressee, someone listening constantly and giving the poet company. In the poem "In the House of Mourning," the widow is the one being studied, for in her, the reader finds the understanding that is needed to contend with death. The widow is defined by her survival—it is she who remains. And Dema identifies with the widow, for through the widow, she explores the dynamics of sexuality, patriarchy, and the strength and capacity of the woman, who, in Dema's hands, remains as strong as she is vulnerable.

> You hear it when widows wake—
> a single name trembling in the night air—
> when you open the door
>
> the look of a lost child
> wanders across her face.
> Only the dead are relieved.
>
> We are left to recollect
> and gather
> what remains
>
> in the house of mourning.

Dema is always aware of the possibility of considering an observation of everyday life as a means of understanding the business of making art and, specifically, of making poems. Those who are left—the widows and the children surviving their parents—are artists, for they "recollect / and gather"—they, in other words, manage memory and find value in the process of re-membering that which has been destroyed and torn apart, and then they gather the "remains."

With Dema, one is best served to offer her the benefit of the doubt as to whether she is punning and alluding to some cultural detail from Botswana, or some classical texts from Greek mythology or the Bible, or some contemporary work of literature or art. She is voracious in her appetite for material that can shape her work, and she is deft in the manner in which she alludes to this rich store of understanding and beauty. In "The Parable of the Tree" for instance, a poem that could be characterized as an activist commentary on the environment, her allusions range from an explicit reference to an article in *Le Monde*; the book of Genesis; George Berkeley, the Irish bishop and philosopher; and Van Gogh. They are compactly managed, never ostentatious, and playfully and smartly enriching our engagement with her ideas. This happens throughout the collection. Dema feels no constraints when it comes to her sources and the substance of her engagement with literary tradition.

TJ Dema is a poet who is as interested in writing about being a poet as she is in writing about her life, war, suffering, sexuality, politics, and much else. Yet one senses a creative intelligence at work in these poems. Blessedly she does not burden us with poems that constantly prat on about the poet. Instead, her collection is laced with what can best be termed ars poetica—and yet the truth is that those poems are serving more than the conceit. They are serving some emotional truth, some ideological idea that she is engaged with. In "Fish Camp," for instance, having taken us through the challenges of having a brother who struggles with his own demons (likely mental illness), she offers us a tender moment of the two siblings fishing on a jetty. This moment is elegant in its own right and serves the collection beautifully. But in the final moment of the poem, it is clear that the "lot" with which she is happy is not just the contentment with being a less than successful fisher but with the difficulties of her art or her poetic vocation.

I am happy with my lot
though I have caught nothing,
save the urge to cast for hours and hours
fishing for something with what I've got.

Dema's similes and metaphors do not announce themselves. Instead, they arrive with the command that comes when language seems inevitable—necessary. This is a quality of maturity and generosity in the poet whose commitment is to contain ideas and feelings in language that clarifies and complicates—a kind of quest for truth. This does not mean her work is simple—it is hardly that. Indeed, Dema is as intrigued by the distractions and befuddlement that come to the reader as she is by the revelatory moments. In "Vesta" the compactness of her imagery is impressive. But note how a suggestion of mystery remains as a mother escapes with her children from an undesirable marriage:

> but we ran
> you tucked into mother's back
> like a small story
> in her sad
> scared mouth

The sacredness and sadness of the mother's mouth are softly and necessarily contradictory, but they capture effectively the vulnerability and strength that draws Dema back to her mother, or, perhaps more accurately, to *the* mother figure.

"The Careless Seamstress" is a splendid conceit for the work that Dema is embarked on. Her collection is filled with voices—particularly those of women, and, at times, the first person speaker may well be Dema herself, or it may be some other body that she is occupying. Still, above everything else, she is collecting buttons, talismans, if you will, for each curse that has come her way from the man in her life. The seamstress who is at once a poet even as she is a woman in a narrative about abuse, about the jealousies of men, and about the independence of a woman in shaping her own economic independence is beautifully painted such that she is able to allow the conceit to unfold without ostentation and alarm. Dema's remarkable narrative lyricism is achieved through her management of the line, her care for detail, and her understanding of the art of selectivity.

The first shirt I made for a stranger
sent my husband into a frenzy,
he likened the minutiae of each stitch
to the way a woman might give her body
to a total stranger.
    Men are saying your name in the marketplace,
    like unrepentant lovers after a common whore.

I've kept a button for every unkind word;
    Witch
    Careless
    Whore.

For Dema, the poet becomes one who is separated from the world and yet who remains defined by and consumed by the world. Her desire to make art is constantly being interrupted by those who do not make art but who, ironically, become the subject of her art. Empathy, then, is not a pious virtue—it is forced on the artist in reach of beauty. One can't fail to see Dema's sense of sardonic humor in this moment in which art seems to arrive for the poet. We must follow the well-made trail she has left—the conceit of the poet as a seamstress; a careless one, who is not deluded into thinking of her labors as especially noble.

A woman knows the way things puncture and hold.
It may be there are men who are strangers to mourning
perhaps the woman too who comes to claim her dress
and twirls and twirls in her matching scarf.
She loves to stop and chat while looking in the glass,
her tattle an old machine stinging my quiet,
blind to the constant fabric under my finger.
To the country of another's distress.

The thing, though, is that while this poet does inhabit the country of another's distress, she is also able to occupy, with poise and skill, the distresses of her own existence. In this, she proves to be generous as she offers language for us to contain the challenges that she sees in her life.

In "The Three-Body Problem" she writes with tenderness and inter-rogative delicacy the story of a brother and a mother. The speaker lays out the challenge of his life, of how he occupies the mind and heart of the mother and the speaker, and yet just how much the core struggle rests in the mother, in what it means to mother a man who is clearly struggling with life—having gone through ten doctors. Dema arrests us so movingly in this description of the pain she is exploring here:

All those years we chased the silence together,
watching from inside something moving along
as fast as my brother's throat could open—
his head thrashing against whatever wall was closest.

We are not sure exactly what he is going through, but the violence, the uncertainty, the silence, these are so effectively captured. And then in the end, the speaker considers what will happen when her mother is no longer there to spend "all her life on him," to perfect her "language of worry," leaving the reader with something of mystery that is, at the same time intuitively clear: "Will I," she asks, "collect cans for his counting?" The dignity she retains in this telling of a man whose struggles consume him is impressive.

She brings this same dignity to bear on another country of distress—that of a girl seeing her first period in the short poem, "Not No Body."

the sheet's bloody tie and dye
that first morning
a mother covering it up quickly
slowing her tongue only to say
that I had to be careful now

and I felt betrayed
as though my body had wandered off
while I slept

and to not feel the blood pulsing
like waking up after the war has ended
all carnage and no story

The image of a body leaving her and returning as something else is brilliantly conceived and then rendered, and then the turn of phrase "all carnage and no story" is rich with humor and terror at the same time.

The last sequence of poems in this collection explores with sophistication the issues of faith and belief through the lens that can best be called agnostic. These poems echo some of the poems that appear earlier in the collection. Dema plays at various kinds of Christian engagements, from being Catholic in "Lent" and "White Noise" to being a witness of evangelical abuses in "On Saying There Is No God," and all of these tested by a deep sense of womanism—a woman's critique of patriarchal constructions that are manifest in the church and elsewhere. Perhaps the most disturbing and timely of these poems is "Stole (Chain of Sorrow)," in which she recounts the pedophilic actions of priests. Dema eschews sensationalism but is willing to explore the weighty implications of this kind of abuse—the institutional failings and, above all, the human failings. She allows herself to speak in the voice of the priests, even as she maintains the critical distance necessary for censure:

One says,
What I gave to a cheerful boy in my youth
cannot be undone—
I live as proof of this.

This is a complex construction, for the undoing is of course a reference to the boy who was abused, the victim, but it is also the abuse the priest enacts on himself, such that the priest is proof of the canker of this act of violence. The passage is then followed by the mantra of abuse and disturbing power, and therefore locates the core of the failing, the heart of the travesty. It is about power; it is about trust; and it is about the shattering of the sacred and the holy.

The boy in the man says,
What the man of god says holds.

When he says drink—then *this* is the way to heaven.

When he says touch—then *his* is the hand of god.

The book says seven—seven—is the age of reason.

We say reason and mean culpability.

In the churchyard—vestments bright as day—
beside the swings where the children play,

one man says, say dying was only a game,
the preacher's cold hand inside your childish pants.

The lines are heartbreaking in their tough assessment of things. In the line "we say reason and mean culpability," the twisted logic of those abusers who seek to excuse their acts is captured with succinct and devastating accuracy.

The Careless Seamstress is an impressive and authoritative debut collection. The maturity of vision and the well-honed craft demonstrated here remind us of just how much work TJ Dema has given to creating a work of importance and power. Dema has effectively brought into the discussion of contemporary African poetry yet another series of ideas and considerations that can only enrich it. Above all, however, this collection ensures that readers and lovers of African poetry from all around the world can have access to the work of a truly gifted voice.

ACKNOWLEDGMENTS

Thanks are due to the editors of the following publications in which these poems first appeared, sometimes in different form.

Cordite Poetry Review: "Benediction for Climbing Boys," "White Noise"

The New Orleans Review: "Naomi," "Sea"

Lyrikline: "Dreams"

Seven New Generation African Poets: A Chapbook Box Set: "At the Last Sound," "Before the Wedding," "Just Because," "Lethe," "Mutineer," "Ovaria," "You Who Have Forgotten"

For their support: my family, Tom Pow, Chris Abani, Matthew Shenoda, Moroka Moreri, Gofamodimo Lekaunyane, Wame Molefhe, Lauri Kubuitsile, the Tea Ladies, Studio Revolt, Ladan Osman, the Lonely Voices Ladies, Phil Rotz, Annie Freud, Word 'n' Sound, Lesego Nchunga-Mokaila, and Mandisa Mabuthoe, the University of Nebraska Press, Slapering Hol Press, and Mary Sibande.

I am grateful to the Department of English and Creative Writing at Lancaster University, the African Poetry Book Fund editorial board and my siblings there, the University of Iowa's International Writing Program, the Danish International Visiting Artists Programme as well as the Alice Kaplan Institute for the Humanities at Northwestern University for time and support.

Thanks to Kwame Dawes—who knows all things—for your ear and your generosity.

Thank you, Kirk Sides, for everything.

THE CARELESS SEAMSTRESS

The Elegy of the Half-Done Quilt

Sisters, do you remember that painting of you with the camellias in your hair,
the one father painted then set alight on the patio to provoke our mother?

Killing time in the attic I find a canvas covered in a dusty quilt, the word *Sor*—
unfinished? Remember how she was always spinning?

Not for her the bright light of wanting, more the dull repetition of being
grateful for each pin prick. A quiet reminder she was alive.

What do you see? There is a mother's shape in the dust settling in that garret.
There she is bent over the candlelight, prom dress draped over her knee.

She was a woman who knew what to do with her hands, how to stitch fabric,
to baste the zip in a new widow's mourning clothes.

More than once I saw her tack a tiny gown for some infant's christening
then turn to make perfect the backstitch for a funeral pall.

Here is a woman who ripped her new stitches hurrying to place a button
or batting on time, to pad three layers each for her daughters' wedding quilts.

Since we were never our mother who knew that a woman's beauty lies
in her hands, most days her tongue worked to drag us up the stairs when

all we wanted to be was downstairs like our daddy. Anything but the
thankless sitting and sitting and you two weeping *I don't want to*

while your boyfriends waited by the curb—I never said a word—
imagined she wanted us to be just like her. We never could have

done half the things she did. She is in there now, in the room the cloth makes for her three daughters to crawl under and finally say

We peddled in small betrayals
Making a mockery of such love
We are sorry we never said sorry

To clasp if not her hands then each other's. Remember her one milky eye
steady as a surgeon's hand, her pursed mouth saying *say sorry to your sister.*

It's what you say to someone you love.

Apoptosis

It seems I have always sat here watching men like you.
—Rita Dove, "From the Sidelines"

Better than the telling was how nothing different happened.
I watched the men at dawn and at sunset
they came in, voices hacking against the night.
None of them accepting the hot bath the women prepared,
they prepared it carefully anyway.

No thought for the early walk to fetch water,
nor the back's quiet ache after years of babies
and a heavy bucket drooling on the head.
The tap a small stick in the horizon.

They were happy—
or so it seemed sometimes—
singing while they gathered *motswere* for fire in the woods.
Collecting dry cow dung to fashion mud bricks,
glad to do it while the men were gone doing god knows what.

Sometimes there was money and
most times there was the women ploughing,
laying stooks heavy as their husbands by hand
and before the reaping their spare figures—
cheap scarecrows—chasing *Quelea* in the light.

Arms collapsing after a day spent between the infant
and what the infant or the bird would eat.
All that sweating for men who thought them gossips,
told on them while they lay between the legs of other wives.

Is it telling how a man will unzip his trousers
barely turning to piss in front of young girls?
I tried to stand neatly in the hut's shadow but
I'd seen the men be kind when they wanted
to put their hands on something to suckle or chew on.

And I was always in trouble for gazing back,
never eating supper till the weekend
when the men would never come home.
Not once I'd seen them gob at the fire

maybe their way of being clean,
as they opened their mouths
raising ash and phlegm into the air.
Better the wood than your feet the women would say
as though *I* should have tried harder.

Red

That first time,
not quite red, maybe brown,
a rusty bloom, its color inchoate
through the morning sheet.

Knowing mother,
no sports now,
no fence jumping with the boys.

A chest bloating with knuckle-sized blossoms,
a waist shrunk
else somewhere else has widened.

Your own body betrays you,
taut as itself aches a bloody ache,
coalesce and collapse, congeal, curdle
a face all cheeks.

A constant blooming,
a forest of gnarled southern trees,
a change as clockwork,
the taste of rust
and old iron in the air,
the mouth a strange thing.
It *says* one thing and opens to let another in.

Geography

In Darvaza a fire has been burning since 1971,
someone's math was off
by about four decades and counting.
On that dresser is a photo,
in it I stand just outside the stave of light an old TV casts in a darkened room.
Next to me is a man who thought I might burn and stay.
I have been touched by fire before,
my skin kindles when I think of it
let's leave it there.

You cannot measure memory in distance,
what will that help
the slow curl and blister of feeling hulled now?
I know what it's like to hold your breath
until there is nothing left to hold you up.

Let's walk backward,
how we arrive here is through greed
the quick bus of body and lust.
Everyone wanting more and more of the brightness
of blood.
The doctor's fingers to my quiet breaths,
we measure what we can, he and I, and leave the rest
to the man shape in the hospital door.
Smoke still rising from his darkened overalls.

In Darvaza someone set up a rig, see the photo—
this is where we surround it with a camp
drill and drill and are surprised
when a pocket of air collapses into a crater.

We were always uncertain
what would do away with us, watch us dig
where we begin to end.
We are prairie and kindling
so someone sets a fire first.

Atropos

I have cut many cloths
thumbed cheap Crimplene
vicuna wool and eiderdown

I have dressed a corpse before
as a child
and again as a bride

I have cut cloth by the yard
to hand stitch a whole skirt in minutes

I have searched for lost skeins
fingers a flock of wild geese
feeding on the studio's cement floor

I have wasted light
chasing redress from parishioners
and men of the cloth

I have sat right here with Leroy the tongue
his one mistress and an angry wife

I have cut many cloths
stabbed infants with glass head pins and
patched a dress halfway to the prom

joints swollen
I tacked a drunk groom's inseam
moments before our wedding song

Taxonomy

No telling what it is, until I cannot lay my palm flat on breastbone.
What knows the shape of a body, better than a wrist and its fingers,
I don't have.

So I stand a hand sideways, thumb on what once was long sternum.
I mean it to fall, hand on heart, not on the plump hill of a breast!

Each morning my palm will look below, to the rough garden of hair.
Search for the old snake in its curly and unlikely watering hole.

But I am diviner now. I dowse for water with my own shaky hand.
I've seen what awaits me. Each month made a wet punishment.

Or a choice between breasts sore from unused milk or the child's
sharp teeth, tight as the ache of fiber and tape set against ribs
to de-form the breast.

My wife calls me by name, Tiresias! Only then am I fully afraid.
To be summoned in the world as a woman, is no small thing.

The Borderlands

I.

In this crowded marketplace
how can there be desire to wet the body?

II.

The soldiers in their camouflage,
the one who says *papers*
and means *what currency do you offer* knows
a young girl can try her tongue and fail but
her body knows silence is a language
any woman can learn to speak.

III.

Far away from here the first initiates' song says
the widening of hips comes with such promise—
not one witness to whisper,
yet its only yield is anguish.

What are we who gawk at the thing
caught in that nightmare?

IV.

For a song the soldier knows
what she'll let him have,
when he says *papers*, his eyes barely search her hands.

In another life I knew the words to say
to a man like this, but here, his eye is the wind
it lifts up her skirt like a broken umbrella.

I turn to cover the children's eyes with my words.
My skin not opaque enough, her face made bright
as a lamp.

V.

Across the border a small sun is rising.
As though the eye were a bridge and the body
were meant to atlas awkwardly
beneath the weight
of its pull.

Ventriloquist

So this is what is left after the party heaves itself outside
while the aunties mumble about vacations and
returning in the family way. Before you do, I say
He won't be able to take much time off work

you see. In my rush to show I understand,
the long dress you insisted on grasps at something,
jerks me back. My little toe catches on rattan
and your eyes say *not again*,

not *sorry*, and I come undone.
That one small tear spilling from my purse:
a narrow tube of lipstick, one tampon,
the dry cleaner's receipt, his sweaty currency

returned to me, the chemist's vial of antihistamine
to stop me sneezing all over your rented trouser
and jacket. To your impatient face I say sorry,
gather the fallen freesias as remnants of pride,

the one card with my old name still on it.
I stumble upright and feel as though I were
the washing machine you thought too fat
to fit in y/our new house. My father offers

a final gift, the bluebook you've coveted
of all his cars. You show me your teeth,
your hand suddenly at my waist says
let everything happen to you.

Even when the callers come to send us off,
their hands full of rice and good wishes,
I bargain for your affection. Smiling at
everything I wonder what to say.

You in your black suit and I in my paper-
white dress am dreaming of a new family tree.
Your mouth twists with disdain. Even the office girl
who does not like me much, eats my sorrow

when you make me say *okay* to the friend
whose voice clatters down our hotel corridor.
Beckoning you to come out and play.
And you do. You do.

Ellen West

who wants to be fat
not I
nor the lady patiently twirling
whose waist disappears
whenever she faces away
or leans over the loo
I'm sure she does
when no one is looking
no one can eat and stay the same
I have tried

falling off a horse

I kissed a child with scarlet fever

a woman died of cold
I stood trying after a winter's bath

yet I am still here weighing sins
putting on and not losing flesh

the girl next door had a child
and lost the baby fat again
I see the weight of men's eyes on her

I promise I'm eating again
though the food sits like a stone

a meal is always on the horizon
a skillfully missed lunch quickly becomes supper
and when we wake there is the food again

am I not one person
my body asks and asks for
then refuses food
thin as skin I tell the doctor
I've tried eating
vegetables
only less and yes
my husband knows
about the laxatives
how I've not bled for years
the cost of one too many pills
but I want a baby so
I am eating again though eating
is dying slowly
why does no one else see it
at ten I moved in the world as a child does
at thirty-three my body is a scene of carnage
it seems nothing
will stop all this eating
not even the heaviness of wanting
to be thin

Ekphrasis

There is nothing to say except that
she is not even singing anymore,
just cross-legged on the floor,
a run on each stocking,
tracks up and down her arms,
shaky cigarette held almost still
between thin cylinder fingers,
and that face, my god!,
that too, everything here but gone:
smile, halo, everything in gray scale
and rain dripping down a felt hat heavy with itself.
You can't imagine this place
or how she's given away all her sitting
to some long-ago boys
and their goddamn vows,
and how is this the answer?
I do not know and I do not know
if somewhere far away from here
some boy has a chisel and hammer
smashing softly into the tiles
of some house he meant to build
for someone like her.

Vesta

father used to place mother
in a three-legged pot
all day she would stew
beneath its cast iron lid
a turtle carrying the world
at night he would free her
and she would sweep and cook
until he was clean and fed
only then would she eat
dampen the hearth and lie
beneath the lid's black weight
and soon another day began
all day she stood singing
and sewing and cleaning
inside that pot

once
on the hottest day of the year
while she was sleeping
a child popped out
of a pumpkin seed
eventually father found out
about the baby
he didn't concern himself
with children or cooking
so long as the work
went on as before
and she thought
    I have to find a way out
    of this pot
    it's too small for two of us

it was years before she could
leave and by then
you too had come along

the night she made father food
put *moselesele* in his soup
he spent hours squatting
in the bush then fell asleep
before closing the lid
all we had
was a bag of seeds
and a way to make fire
but we ran
you tucked into mother's back
like a small story
in her sad
scared mouth

Nostalgia

Johannesburg, 1994

My father who came here as a miner from Botswana
    Stayed for love of a life and love
He hated Christmas in this old country
    The tin-house heat and sporadic rain
Till the day he died of lung disease he complained
    The storm always came unannounced
And I'd say not for the man who stands at the control tower
    Nor the woman whose scar itches before it rains or
The swallows who sweep the sky in warning

What is left is only ever what is returned for
    Memory is mist you wade through toward
A childhood friend whose name you no longer remember
    I promise myself this visit will be longer
That every relative will call me old and tire of my face
    That we will stand hands in pockets in the same spot
Our childish tongues licked ice pops and played "black mampatile" on
    This time in mulberry silk yelling nothing's changed

When the woman with the microphone turns to me
    I do not see her or her question coming
I want to say how happy we were
    The girls' braids so tight they could not sleep
How we sneaked outside to lean against the iron wall
    Its corrugated nudge warm rust against us
But I suddenly know what she means to hear
    The way a mother's slap might rain down unannounced
Or a man die for walking these streets without a pass

The Careless Seamstress

> When she thinks of what is the one constant
> in her life, she thinks of the stitch.
> —Virgil Suarez, "The Seamstress"

At first of course the bloody loop breaks
again and I think my husband likes
how I sit and sew,
then repeat myself,
fat thumb pressed to flat-tipped finger.
A steel vein carrying thread where it's needed,
needle to cloth and the sweeping out of wrinkles
from fabric and sweaty face.

   You are a good wife,
he would say,
   not taking on man's work.
Comforted by my sense of place
in staying at home to sew and sew,
a missing button here,
the torn pocket there,
to work without work

at labor's pew.

The first shirt I made for a stranger
sent my husband into a frenzy,
he likened the minutiae of each stitch
to the way a woman might give her body
to a total stranger.
   Men are saying your name in the marketplace,
   like unrepentant lovers after a common whore.

I've kept a button for every unkind word;
   Witch
   Careless
   Whore.
My vase is full with flats and studs and toggles,
with shanks and mismatched poppers,
I think of Joseph's coat—the one the preacher mentioned.
I am faithful as a nun and must forgive though he does not
confess to anything.

A woman knows the way things puncture and hold.
It may be there are men who are strangers to mourning
perhaps the woman too who comes to claim her dress
and twirls and twirls in her matching scarf.
She loves to stop and chat while looking in the glass,
her tattle an old machine stinging my quiet,
blind to the constant fabric under my finger.
To the country of another's distress.

The Three-Body Problem

i

When we are finally aboard the train
    to see the tenth doctor some neighbor recommends
no one will speak to me.
I ferret for attention,
lean on our mother but she pendulums   away.

There are many things a little boy might want—
what does that make anyone imagine—
a favorite toy   perhaps a blanket?

When I close my eyes
I want to see my mother sitting down
yet when she does   she is always a film of sweat.

And just like the story you may hear
about a sick aunt who comes to visit
and never leaves
all of my childhood   my sick aunt
was my older brother.
He would flap his arms about and mother would stand rushing,

he always needed something;
someone to look at him while he would look at no one.
I wondered what expanse drew him within,
above atlas and cheekbone—
who does not move to the sound of his own name?

To avoid mayhem,
cans emptied quickly from the shelf so he could stack them

one by one and over and over again.
And on the train   none of the things a boy like this might need.

ii

He is her life's work—
for now—
when I offer respite
he and I wander the corridors worrying
at whatever keeps his mind here.

A neighbor might see his bruised body and call the police,
an officer might try to find where the bruising began,
on these days I know the tense buckle of mother's knees.
When the doorbell rings I am clasping the edge of her hem.
I am well my scars invisible.
Once when a neighbor fed her wine
mother called her son,
     a constant train of events.
Everything has its limits,
she said,
     his silence is a ticking clock.

iii

All those years we chased the silence together,
watching from inside something moving along
as fast as my brother's throat could open—
his head thrashing against whatever wall was closest.

On that train ride,
long ago,
mother would not wipe her own wet face.
I imagine

there are many things a mother might want,
perhaps the same son   a workable silence.

He has grown calmer with age.
She has spent all her life on him.

When she is gone,
who will inherit her language
of worry,
        his silence,
will I collect cans for his counting?

Lent

The year I played at being Catholic
I lamented how slowly the weeks moved
toward Holy Saturday;
the baker complaining—
no one buys bread anymore—
the merchant's cellars full with wine.
All day I was hungry for more than food.

And on the walk home not once did the girl I liked
say anything as the tar turned to sand
and the road narrowed to potholes and dirt.
Two bodies hummed loudly in the quiet night.

Hunger sharpened wanting
intention slowly turned to ash in the mouth,
so we lifted our palms and touched briefly,

until the cant of a mother
on a not-dark-enough street
measured the distance between us.

Not No Body

and before we did not think of ourselves
as bodies
even when I stuffed an old sock to make
one odd breast
everyone laughed
it was all apery

I did not know
the sheet's bloody tie and dye
that first morning
a mother covering it up quickly
slowing her tongue only to say
that I had to be careful now

and I felt betrayed
as though my body had wandered off
while I slept
and to not feel the blood pulsing
like waking up after the war has ended
all carnage and no story

you could wash sheets of course
turn over the hard bed
with its new birthmark
pretend none of it had happened
I was horrified
though no one would let me be

the whole time my aunt was saying
hallelujah on the phone
her sister looked a little terrified
and I was praying my cousins
her boys
were still drunk with milk and sleep

Women Like You

hold the sharp end of a knife,
bottles scattering in the wake of children
and morning life.

This is the contract.

To make in the shadows
and in the light, settle
for things like breath and bread,

while inside you clamor
as the eyes of drunk men
touching the young girl walking.

As hunters would
your days will dig a trapping pit
where you and she might emerge,

your hands bloody with practice.

Dreams

Dreams are evil.
I prefer nightmares.
They show you what goes on in here,
reflects what goes on out there.

Dreams lie.
They lead you down a path
where white chocolate flows undammed,
and mulberries fall unshaken from the trees.

Nothing is less faithful,
less real,
or more untrue than a dream.

And does every waking moment have to be so hard?
I am tired of spending sleepless nights
chasing hesitant tomorrows, biding my time
just to spend it mending broken things
that have no wish to be fixed.

I will not spin and spin inside this skin.
I will not mourn a future I never had.
I refuse to bleed myself
for an almost reality rooted in the distant echoes
of a once familiar voice
chanting I know I can, I know I can.
Because I know I can
be the girl I am right now,
live the life I have right now,
choose to be the dream I am in right now.
Maybe then it won't be so hard
just to breathe right now.

Ovaria

Women know
that sometimes there is blood
but not death; they learn
to conceal the womb with breasts,
to choose that which can be lost—
the hopeful recipe or the constant
cake in cupboard—
to empty their cup,
and to be content
with utterly nothing.

Before the Wedding

Your dog has eaten our eggs.
Bent more than slightly at waist and knee,
he sways into the sturdiest looking chair.
Though he broke her good leg,
smashed our prized gourd,
she says they played together.

Everyone knows a cow will undo the damage.

They send a bevy of beards,
gravel-voiced, gray-haired coat wearers,
who speak in song without the drum,
hum as many though they employ only one tongue.

The guests who have come to make family of her clan ask,
Will the calf carry our name?
If so, we are the wood come to right the kraal our bull careened through;
we have come to own this joyful mistake,
to add to our numbers a daughter.
This is our purpose, in asking for the hand of the bearer,
she who carries our water.

Lethe

This is not that river
portico filled with wet shadow
and sand.
This is deciduous memory,
and it grates against
whatever remains
whatever reasons,
designs we have concealed.
Each day concedes there is nothing
not one thing to take away from here.
Yet we make work of shredding everything,
and our hands clutching at round river rock
tell us that some things stay
rooted as gingko on the bank
while others erode into the current.
Come tomorrow you will not know
why you cannot forget
dogmata of fairy tale
or from adult memory
erase the giver of this drink
whose fluorescent face
turned your tactile midnight form
to foam
in that loud morning light.

Mutineer

I have been spotted
spreading one leg toward the light

They come for me
while I am naked as desert sand

Wet behind ear / I am rain
between thighs / I am forest growing everything anew

I am sand slipping away the fullness of youth
I have grown gills in the name of a storm coming

You Who Have Forgotten

When you were born,
my body tore itself open.

To hold you I unfolded every seam,
let them snip and unspool me.

For weeks I bled because of you
and banished laughter to the periphery of memory.

To reach the rooms where you can send
no one but yourself,
I sat in salt, crawled,
and padded my threaded belly
together with the thought of you.

After tonight's grand performance,
you are mistaken
to think I could not take back
the life that I have given.

Just Because

Because I know you are going to ask
where the flowers are,
I have picked roses red and sweet,
left them by the wayside for the birds to eat.

Because I know you are going to ask
where the sweets are,
I have made you *halwa* with these hands
stirred and then spilt what was yours.

Because I know you are going to ask
where I am,
I have long left the place I was
to walk slow between the trees

where your greedy eye cannot reach me.

At the Last Sound

for Gabeba Baderoon

If there was a place where nothing was at first,
there is everything here now

At last the sound of your voice
so soft, yet though I try to

I cannot liken the inevitable avalanche
of a thickening whisper to

You

are gossamer
grain blown, then evened into glass
    smooth
      though you do not mean to be

      anything but yourself. I am dreaming
      always of being next to the body of sound

      your voice makes.

Winter Tortoise

At first light you are biting nails
seemingly ill at ease.
Last night your familiar song
of stay one more day
was met with a final yes.

Now you have us all looking
for a ring. We look though we know
that you are searching for that thing
that can only be found by the one
who put it where it is now.

You water the colocasia,
too big now to stay indoors.
But who can imagine burying one more thing,
especially this—his last gift—
between whose foliage you now rummage,
peeking between the leafy shadows.

Eventually you stand still,
spill to the room's only couch.
You blink,

lucid inside the white noise of memory,

too many helpful hands foraging.

Anyone who cares to,

watches your eyes follow the light—

specks of dust buoyant and diagonal—

wondering if you'll ever find it.

Your heart has lost its home.

As though your name were called,

you rise up one last time.

Domboshaba

Imagine you come from this
familiar everyday of corn and air
your dead hurled overboard
without the ceremony
of leaving in peace,
finally the vertigo of rising to some foreign shore.

Imagine you come from this
and then you wake up
in a shack
on a sugar plantation.

You are hungry
for the open air
yet unable to name the thing
not there anymore.

Dennis Brutus says of a different prison,
It is not all terror
and deprivation.

Between their redemption and your salvation,
you will walk to a drum song,
its skin fraught with wickedness;
but this rock above you now folds and folds and
folds, holding the ancient, the future, and the you
standing here now on the edge of it all.

Self-Portrait with a Missing Tongue

Monna ga a botswe kwa a tswang teng

It is only that I am afraid I will swallow my tongue,
forget the sound of my own voice;
that one day you will ask me my name and I will go to dust
the ash off my tongue.
Only where will my tongue be
in this portrait of perfectly tied scarves and
sweeper's backs bent over noisy fires.

Perhaps my mouth will be holy
but empty as the man who said thrice he did not know his savior.
Who amongst us knows whether our mothers truly favor silence
or whether the price of asking a man where he has been
is far greater than the shame of knowing?

Here are the thirty pieces of silver
to give the earth back her open mouth.
I will plant them, lay them on the forest floor
so the enemy will not come up behind you,
and I without a tongue
with which to say
anything.

A Benediction for Climbing Boys

Sometimes the chimney was hot or alight.
They sent us up anyway, mostly naked.
At night we, sleeping black,
dreamt of the bakers on Lothbury,
of tight flues and endless winding.

The first time Jonny went up,
there was not even four years behind him.
He was up while the chimney was cold,
before the morning fire was lit. His skinny limbs,
cramped, waited for the mason's cutting tools.

Luck for the bride who sees us perhaps.
We are blind with slack and dust.
We are burnt and scraped, our knees
set to fire with brine and brush
to harden our small hearts.

In the fairy tales, the sweep finds love
with a porcelain shepherdess.
After May Day, we are turned from the table
to which we return, for the world
gifts us only sack cloth and ashes.

*

There is no cap coarse enough
to keep the soot from eye or mouth,
no talisman of brass cap badges
to shame the master who sends them up
to fall from roofs and chimneys,

to lodge in flues and suffocate.
Whose son has fire set under him
his heels pricked to mend his pace?
This is the cold fate of he who is alone,
whose mother has died, left his body

for the world to take and make coal.
And whose back is bent in youth
his scrotum set to eat itself away?
We die knowing what is denied us:
air and love, a clean wanting.

Shibboleth

What trap awaits us I think I know.
You cannot have one without the other.
Belonging creates unbelonging.

And so much seems intent on separation
Somewhere between body and blood,
something remains as a good fence,

or color at the shaver's sink.
My father's face unshaven
all these weeks at sea

shifts the borders of posture,
the way you lean a face over seething water
to sweat the sick out of you.

This is for the devout drowned
whose tongues lick tangled seaweed,
who rise beautiful from some ocean floor

with the wakefulness of a clean face,
the soused in white wet robes on the shore,
when everywhere else is the river Jordan.

Before we pull any or all eight
hundred and eighty out of the sea,
they must say *water*,

swallow the slosh of a soft *r*,
the imagined ridge of a letter *d*
in place of the water's dry *t*.

Sea

he must've thought   what a sight
the first to see us
fishing net in hand   his sailor's eyes   crow's feet   pulling
at his furrowed brow
I suppose the sun was before
or
behind us   and he was on his way home
to a bowl of muddy coffee
or
heading out to sea

who knows what wakes him now   each day before morning
having seen what he saw

I'm sure of it
or would be   if I were still here

a boat full of bodies
    must change the shape of a horizon so

The Parable of the Tree

The maximum permissible CO_2 limit was crossed just before 1990.
   —*Le Monde*, 7 May 2013

this is not a forest, no
it is a tree, and then another
in which a chipmunk lives his whole life unknowing

there is a matter concerning earth
   and man and why
the forest is suddenly at a crossroads

why should he not pick fruit from the troubled tree,when it is not
   he   who troubles the tree—

it with its bounty of fruit   and him
with no pocket   only a cheek full of nuts

while his neighbor   whose field is a basket of gold
parades his gaiety in these woods

*

say the tree is only a tree   what makes air
for the man who holds his breath
longer than the thud of a falling oak

tell the man who cuts off   his own ear   as though it were wheat
that what he has summoned
has finally come.

Mama

If I turn back I can see you
lying on the train floor.
Never a rambler you must've been
sleeping off time spent herding
or milking or yanking cornstalks
out of the defiant ground.
Your one good dress is rubbing its paisley
between teenage skin and dusty floor,
the train's constant chug
a strange lullaby for all those years
you slept through the night
then woke up just before
the first day of school
made itself known.
That one time you couldn't find your shoe
though you looked everywhere
and searched and searched,
you left the train with only one shoe.
And the uncle you wrote to was an unbeliever
in fathers who sent daughters off,
without a way to make it
through boarding school.
If it wasn't for the girl
who gave you her sandals
to wear to class
or the nuns whose rules
meant everyone wore blue,
whose mother would you be?

In the House of Mourning

I. FIRE

We've practice enough at grieving.

Perhaps fire is right,
let us burn everything and be done with it.

II. WIDOW

In the distance a shape she recognizes
but cannot name. The threat of it enough
to send a bowl of flour flying.

A boy of five or six twirls like a maple seed,
making a whirlwind of the falling cloud
inside his absent father's house—

the dead resurrect
in the faces of their young, ants
fidgeting in the mind's underbrush.

III. WHAT REMAINS

You hear it when widows wake—
a single name trembling in the night air—
when you open the door

the look of a lost child
wanders across her face.
Only the dead are relieved.

We are left to recollect
and gather
what remains

in the house of mourning.

IV. IN THE HOUSE OF MOURNING

Everyone rehearses death,
at nightfall. The rise and fall
of breath taken or withheld

when the hunters return
to the table, reeking of blood
and tales, and one is not amongst them.

The one who liked songs is gone.
Only the dog barks at nothing,
zephyr blowing as it does

at another yellow sky
tucking its skirt in
for the night.

Fetching

Not so much the cow as its hindered hooves,
legs tied together to keep a beast
from straying. More how it gives milk,
its flesh. At the last its hide to cover us.

I cannot say why I stopped,
full metal bucket heavy on head.
My neck yoked to the water's heavy nuisance,
one arm a makeshift brace.

Water comes unwelcome in my dreams too,
why not here? Its jostled body the feel of wet hair,
a river down my back, the sudden mud
of feet as clay.

"Jostling is for beasts, correct your gait."
Here, aunts replace absent mothers,
a necessary nuisance to keep a daughter
from straying. We empty our pails

and are left with the nothingness
of the bucket's open mouth,
as we walk the same fetch past preening boys,
and the breastless girls playing *suna baby*.

On the way back, no patience for the berries
blooming wild on the briary sidelines,
not with the water vat half empty
and the day just done.

My aunt's backward squint at the body
naming me a cow knocking into its grace.
The slow feel of feet, caking dry with mud.
My back still a gorge.

Batting

To begin with
your maiden name was never yours, only that
your father loaned you his own
to tide you through the morning you would wake up,
with women saying exactly this to you.
While you try to return the packed dresses
to their familiar wardrobe and the words to their speakers
you are only one girl. And your aunts are sifting through
old letters stained with rooibos and tears,
photographs from what is fast becoming another life
all this while they mend your favorite quilt.
They carefully stitch its nine-patch blocks,
set aside your books to make room for your new name.

When mother tells you *go*,
go seems so final and far
from the prize giving at school
the handwritten greetings cards.
That one word splices the air between us.

I still see mother's face as the car drives away,
feel how your knees give way when you see the kist;
heavy with its pots and spoons and needles—
a woman's treasure, in this new life.
I whisper your old name one more time, regret you
and I were not born boys
we could keep our names then.

*

I turn eleven and dream of beaks at my liver, bright-mouthed birds
of penance. I wake with blood between my thighs,
when I call to tell you your voice is a frog
on a horse's hoof.
I come around, an old Christmas card and your birth certificate in hand.
With downcast eyes you sit knitting black wool,
you tell me we all go eventually.

That childhood is stitching together
what will be turned to sew together two lives,
that time is a waiting room
from which I cannot ask the obvious.
How a body learns to navigate such straits,
how long it takes to lose a woman from her name—
the answer is:
I know who will be buried far away from home
and whose language the children will speak.

Mourning at Night

I can only mourn my friends at night,
For I am intimate with the moon
And in it many months I've confided.
He who killed me is still at large.
　　—Abdul-Rahman al-Abnudi, "The Usual Sorrows"

He never made it back,
the one made to choose
between a kraal and whatever
fracture till then passed for home.

The thing done was never spoken
out loud, beyond the almost word
occasioned by some fleeting fury
sitting then slipping past a father's tongue.
If you pray eyes closed you cannot see
keloid memory Lazarused back
to some shiny half-life,
only a sudden quiet two generations down
when the partisan cocktail laughter languishes
over a bowl of tiny nuts—
fried until they too shed their first skin.

Sometimes two may stand outside a kraal
and share an unspoken remembrance
before the earth breaks that unnatural bond,
the soil sending message of an impending herd
laying fallow the trudging threat.
The eggshell peace there
only to spell out that there is a thing unsayable,
that for some the cloth across a shoulder,

the tight knit knot of cotton on head
is a way to speak everything that needs saying.

One man, too old now to care who might overhear
looks away as his finger points to land like any other
and says, It was here, amidst the dung and broken wood
that we men saw a woman give birth for the first time.

Once you have slept in a womb
born of your own blood, Madawo
and still borne the stamp of who you are not,
make friends with the noon rain,
scatter bashfulness with the moon wind,
and each morning know to hunt
and gather your true self together again
until the hoofed scale of each cow equates
to a man's freedom.

The one made to choose
between kraal and concourse
never made it back,
for no one falls upon blood
and thinks "I will remain here, cleanly."
How glad are we that they who return
have risen above the din of past tense,
the callused chatter of hindsight.

First Algebra

The bus was a big room full of crying infants
and though I looked back I could not see my mother
nor the little house she rented for us.
A small kid was singing something that needed a choir
when someone yelled shut up and stopped the note in his throat.

First day of school and my tongue trying to learn
the letters that stood in place of the unknown,
the lines you were meant to understand you shouldn't cross.
Everyone laughed when I said water.
I admit I sounded like my father, who had equal talent
for languages as running away from trouble.

Father who loved humming was gone
and there was no one left to explain the boys
who chased you down after school
and how that might follow you all your life,
in the way you said yes to everything.

It all seems so abstract now—
the idea of changing and moving—
how the mind is meant to quietly follow the body.
Like learning human algebra from the back of some room,
the teacher's chalky hand trying to reunite all the broken parts.

The Other

A pale man with a camera says, *Stand here.*
When no one moves he touches Naro,
places us as mannequins one after the other.
When he smiles we understand this much,
he has gotten what he came for.
We may stop dancing now and tend to our actual chores.

The first time I hear the word bushman, the word *Nkhwa,*
I am mostly surprised by the speaker's tone.
The word itself means nothing to me.

We've learnt to answer to *Mosarwa* when people say this,
though this is not what we call ourselves.
It is strange to reconcile calling in a language your dead do not speak.

Most nights I cannot sleep so I stay awake counting the stars.
I worry that when our ancestors come for us they will not know
where to look
for we are so far away from home.
I want the privilege of sleep but I dream
of dismantled huts, loud men, open trucks, and a bumpy road.

We hear whispers that even the city has no water.
Grandfather asks whether they have the Mokate melons
that hydrate our bodies with their drink.

When I see a thing I ask, *What do* you *call this?*
The little girl whose hair has been stretched to within an inch of itself giggles
and says, *You speak funny.*
Despite the strangeness of things, I like many things here.
The new school I go to even has a wide television.

If I make her tea, the teacher lets me sit and watch, for a while.
On one of these days I see a man on the screen.
He is beyond crying and kneeling.
The first thing that catches my eye is the sand seemingly everywhere
all around him.
Finally, I come to rest on the small child lying quietly in his arms.
Behind him an angry sea is spitting out dark-haired bodies
and the wet wood of a broken boat.
The hair on the back of my neck curls into itself. I recognize loss,
I have touched its face before. And this kind of leaving is far too familiar.

Perhaps it is better to sit and drink out of boredom
than to wander a wilderness of sand.
Our strength is weakness here.
These hands know how to make an arrow from the bones of dead animals.
They know when not to hunt the kudu or its young.
But I know too the hand of politics; I am not immune to change.
I am of the man you see painted on rocks but I am also of this time.
My father who knew so much is at a loss.
I have heard the word depression from the woman at the clinic
who gives me sweets when no one is looking.
She says it in the same kind, quick breath as Aborigine and Inuit, as refugee.

My cousin Ki'lo who is walking away from our ways says,
We are not the first people to be moved,
do not be ungrateful, we have schools and a nurse to heal the diseases
we did not even have names for before
and a bottle store, he says, eyes sparkling.
This is our home now.
I can only wonder if a roof is really all it takes to make a home.

My dreams are changing.
At night, I can no longer picture the path I walked every day
as a child. Under this stage of tin roofs and bright lights

it gets harder to remember that there is no blanket
thick enough to keep you warm where you are denied the empathy of
    humanness.
Even the borrowed blankets know.
They too hear the whispered distaste,
so they start to ration their itches like the food we receive monthly,
and cover us in shame.

In the combi the girl who likes mirrors says she is *a Motswana
not Botswanian* and next time the reporter *better get it right.*
I have been taking classes to learn these other words
so when she says *Masarwa a,* I wonder whether she sees herself.
Perhaps she is Janus the two faced who looks both forward
and backward at the same time.
But I fear it is much simpler than that. Most people cannot feel a hurt
that does not look like them, even if it belongs to them.

When the chance to return home is set before us
we finally understand the word *assimilate*. We do.
We reencounter ourselves,
the new lines drawn on faces, between places.
We are changed by geography
as *all* people are
if they survive.

Stole (Chain of Sorrow)

What once was has come again.

The priests summon but cannot keep piety.

One says,
What I gave to a cheerful boy in my youth
cannot be undone—
I live as proof of this.

The boy in the man says,
What the man of god says holds.

When he says drink—then *this* is the way to heaven.

When he says touch—then *his* is the hand of god.

The book says seven—seven—is the age of reason.

We say reason and mean culpability.

In the churchyard—vestments bright as day—
beside the swings where the children play,

one man says, say dying was only a game,
the preacher's cold hand inside your childish pants.

Your whole life—inside—you
would be a howling gale.

In the roundabout's slow twirl another asks,
Who will return to us
all the years the locust has eaten?

Lares

Let us say
his mother died giving birth to him,
and he
still alive
was to be buried with her.

Let me tell you what it's like
to carry a child that's not yours
while you fetch water with a steel bucket pissing on your head.
One more mouth to feed
when many women had their own to contend with,
their world already rich with offspring.

The women did not make the choice lightly
even as they mobbed around the newborn's mother like kind vultures
their wings—shoulders shrouded in funeral blankets.
There was the wailing,
the quiet certainty its father would not ask after the child.

Their hearts hardened.
Resolve is its own path
and path, reason
so kill it
be done with the loss all at once.
For centuries this had been the best way.
Let she who wants to change it
step into this circle with broom and magic to sweep out what is familiar.

The circle held all through the night.

One mother unable to stay the path,
placed the sleeping orphan
upon her own child's back.
To hear him tell it now, she said,
do not hesitate or answer
not even to your own name
even if it is my voice.
No good can come of this hour. She said,
Do not stop until you see the wall that is your grandmother's face.

All through the night and into morning
the momentum of ritual carried the would-be killers through their lonely burial.
They could not, once they had begun burying their sister,
stop the hymns to search for one child—
lost to them either way.
Whoever had stolen away with it had unburdened them
and who could stop the swift song of a boy,
a child strapped to his small back
as he swung through the forest of his childhood
the rite of running barefoot perfected through backways and shrubs
that now whispered to him
faster
then this way
this way.

Fish Camp

I cannot bring myself to spear the shrimp
kept alive in a bucket for just this purpose,
so my brother does the stitching of hook to flesh.

For hours I flick and yank myself
into something resembling rhythm,
still nothing but blowfish and bait bites.

For fifty years this camp has sat here
floating over pylons dug into the sea,
weathering hurricanes and storms,
the gulf lapping angrily at its feet.

I am sitting on its wooden deck
bare feet dangling over cold sea,
nothing but our white boat knocking
like a hesitant neighbor in the night.

I am happy with my lot
though I have caught nothing,
save the urge to cast for hours and hours
fishing for something with what I've got.

Naomi

In the beginning
the chickens have no cause to fear us,
we are all of us far too young to worry.

My sister works well
at the daily chore of keeping everyone alive

while I run circles around the ankles of girls
who've bled like her,
who sit and peel potatoes,

turning wood into fire
time making bellows of their lungs.

They dunk whole chickens in vats of boiling water,
pluck their feathers by hand.

I could never bring myself to watch,
to hold the bird by its neck,
to use its weight against its will to live.

Naomi could swing and sing
the same tune
       she used to

send us off to sleep.
My back turned to where I know I'm headed.

White Noise

What will bear the burden of all that noise?
—Stephen Dobyns

And where is the point
at which penance comes knees bent
your name absolution on its tongue?

We can only hope for something
that knows—perhaps when we do not—
the taste of clemency,
when the sentence is done;

something familiar and new all at once
that tempts us, shows us
these seams are easily undone,
that ink is the hangman

with a forgiving noose.

Each one of us is born sensible
a heart incensed then falling.

We know the white space left
for our open-mouthed cry,
the slow babble of delight.

But now and then we forget
here is the point,
a place to reckon with,

where beneath a crown heavy with words
is a seat of acacia and hawthorn
to say choose carefully the weight
of each syllable upon the tongue.

On Saying There Is No God

I took it all back
when mama dunked my head in a sudden baptism.

She said this almost drowning is next to godliness
and ain't I lucky the price isn't beauty.

She turned the metal tub into a giant teacup,
wiped my soapy mouth clean,

then stared at the plain tunic
the one she meant for me to wear.

Dry as a pew on a weekday I saunter to church,
see how we are all gods,

take the small breeze prayed for
when we are held ransom by heat and Pastor Modisa alike.

Perhaps god is instinct
and instinct memory;

the body's return to knowing
and, what do I know, save mistrust?

I see the way Mma Modisa moves,
her hand a faithful kerchief across her husband's sweaty face.

Who is the baptized when he screams
repent,
repent!
while rivulets roll down his soft face?

Even the child crawling between the unclean pews
is astonished

when no one slaps his black bottom to call him
upward from the hall's newly scuffed woodwork.

Afterward, waiting for mama on the stoop
I count how many walk out to their rented rooms

to gather more penance as tithe for the coming week.
I leave a blank spot for our own quiet trek home.
    Here she comes,

mama, humming what we go do
what we go do about supper now?

Homonym

After Safia Elhillo's "Vocabulary"

the Setswana word madi means blood
the Setswana word madi means money
the minister of finance said   *here is the money*
or
the minister of finance said   *here is the blood*
    the minister waves his hands admits   to touching   money
                     or
    the minister waves his hands admits   to touching   blood

his voice is shaky and for a moment the people do not know which he means

to say

voice   you say lentswe
but to say
stone   you say lentswe

Nkuku's favorite folktale has a giant who swallows   a stone
or perhaps he swallows   a voice
either way his own softens and the little girl   home alone
lets the giant in and is swallowed   whole

in a fight   on the day of the impeachment   my cousin comes home
from England and says   *people who live in glass houses shouldn't throw stones*   but
her accent has shifted, she hefts the words from overseas to home
for a moment she yells
people in glass houses shouldn't throw away their   *voices*

"At the Last Sound" borrows and alters language from Gabeba Baderoon's poetry collection *The Dream in the Next Body*.

"Self-Portrait with a Missing Tongue" uses a Setswana saying as its epigraph, which translates as "never ask a man where he has been." Often recited to a bride-in-waiting by married women as part of traditional premarital counseling.

"Domboshaba" borrows a phrase from Dennis Brutus's poem "Letters to Martha."

"The Parable of the Tree" takes its epigraph as per Bruno Latour's translation of a headline from *Le Monde* in his article "Agency at the Time of the Anthropocene."

"Stole (Chain of Sorrow)" paraphrases the Bible verse Joel 2:25.

"Naomi" borrows and alters its final line from Natasha Tretheway's "Elegy" ("I think by now the river must be thick").

IN THE AFRICAN POETRY BOOK SERIES

Logotherapy
Mukoma Wa Ngugi

When the Wanderers Come Home
Patricia Jabbeh Wesley

Seven New Generation African Poets: A Chapbook Box Set
Edited by Kwame Dawes
and Chris Abani
(Slapering Hol)

Eight New-Generation African Poets: A Chapbook Box Set
Edited by Kwame Dawes
and Chris Abani
(Akashic Books)

New-Generation African Poets: A Chapbook Box Set (Tatu)
Edited by Kwame Dawes
and Chris Abani
(Akashic Books)

New-Generation African Poets: A Chapbook Box Set (Nne)
Edited by Kwame Dawes
and Chris Abani
(Akashic Books)

New-Generation African Poets: A Chapbook Box Set (Tano)
Edited by Kwame Dawes
and Chris Abani
(Akashic Books)

To order or obtain more information on these or other University of Nebraska Press titles, visit nebraskapress.unl.edu. For more information about the African Poetry Book Series, visit africanpoetrybf.unl.edu.

Lightning Source UK Ltd.
Milton Keynes UK
UKHW012010270522
403605UK00011B/281